16

W9-AYM-749

Ready for School
We Follow the Rules

Listos para ir a la escuela
Respetamos las reglas

Sharon Gordon

Marshall Cavendish
Benchmark
New York

We follow the rules.

Respetamos las reglas.

We line up.
We follow the rules.

———————◆———————

Hacemos una fila.
Respetamos las reglas.

We sit down.
We follow the rules.

Nos sentamos.
Respetamos las reglas.

We walk.

We follow the rules.

❖

Caminamos.

Respetamos las reglas.

We raise our hands.
We follow the rules.

––––––––– ❖ –––––––––

Levantamos la mano.
Respetamos las reglas.

We take turns.

We follow the rules.

❖

Nos turnamos.

Respetamos las reglas.

13

We listen.

We follow the rules.

Escuchamos.

Respetamos las reglas.

We wash our hands.
We follow the rules.

Nos lavamos las manos.
Respetamos las reglas.

17

We play.

We follow the rules!

❖

Jugamos.

¡Respetamos las reglas!

We Follow the Rules
Respetamos las reglas

hands
manos

line up
hacer una fila

listen
escuchar

play
jugar

sit down
sentarse

take turns
turnarse

walk
caminar

wash
lavarse

Index

Índice

About the Author
Datos biográficos de la autora

Sharon Gordon has written many books for young children. She has always worked as an editor. Sharon and her husband Bruce have three children, Douglas, Katie, and Laura, and one spoiled pooch, Samantha. They live in Midland Park, New Jersey.

❖

Sharon Gordon ha escrito muchos libros para niños. Siempre ha trabajado como editora. Sharon y su esposo Bruce tienen tres niños, Douglas, Katie y Laura, y una perra consentida, Samantha. Viven en Midland Park, Nueva Jersey.

With thanks to Nanci Vargus, Ed.D. and
Beth Walker Gambro, reading consultants

Marshall Cavendish Benchmark
99 White Plains Road
Tarrytown, New York 10591-9001
www.marshallcavendish.us

Library of Congress Cataloging-in-Publication Data

Gordon, Sharon.
[We follow the rules. Spanish & English]
We follow the rules = Respetamos las reglas / Sharon Gordon. — Bilingual ed.
p. cm. — (Bookworms. Listos para ir a la escuela)
Includes index.
ISBN-13: 978-0-7614-2438-3 (bilingual edition)
ISBN-10: 0-7614-2438-5 (bilingual edition)
ISBN-13: 978-0-7614-2358-4 (Spanish edition)
ISBN-10: 0-7614-1995-0 (English edition)
1. Obedience—Juvenile literature. 2. School children—Conduct of life. I. Title. II. Title: Respetamos las reglas.

BJ1459.G6718 2006b
179'.9—dc22
2006018275

Spanish Translation and Text Composition by Victory Productions, Inc.
www.victoryprd.com

Photo Research by Anne Burns Images

Cover Photo by Corbis/Jim Craigmyle

The photographs in this book are used with permission and through the courtesy of:
Corbis: pp. 1, 11, 20 (top l) Steve Chenn; pp. 3, 5, 20 (top r) Royalty Free; pp. 7, 9, 13, 15, 19, 20 (bottom l),
20 (bottom r), 21 (top l), 21 (top r), 21 (bottom l) Ariel Skelley; pp. 17, 21 (bottom r) Ralf-Finn Hestoft.

Printed in Malaysia
1 3 5 6 4 2